YET WILL I TRUST HIM

A Sedonia Roland Memoir

KASSAUNDRA HESTER

YET WILL I TRUST HIM

A Sedonia Roland Memoir

KASSAUNDRA HESTER

Yet Will I Trust Him
A Sedonia Roland Memoir

©2024 Kassaundra Hester

print ISBN: 979-8-35097-654-0
ebook ISBN: 979-8-35097-655-7

DEDICATION

*This book is dedicated with love and affection to my brothers and
sisters, Zelda, Terrance, Derrick, Lonnie Jr, John Jr, Jeri, Sophia,
Timothy, Talvin and Lonnette. God has placed a special bond
in my heart for each of you. You have provided the inspiration
needed to finally bring this milestone to fruition. I am forever
grateful for the many memories we have made while exploring
this thing called life together. If there is one thing I would like
for you to remember is to always keep God as the head of your
life. Your obedience will allow Him to birth the unimaginable
out of you, so walk in V-I-C-T-O-R-Y and know that you
are more than a conqueror through Him that loved you.*

CONTENTS

Chapter 1:

GROWING UP
IN THE SOUTH

∽∽∽∾∽∽

omans 8:18 (KJV): "For I reckon that the suf-
ferings of this present time are not worthy to
be compared with the glory which shall be revealed in us."

I HAVE OFTEN WONDERED WHAT MY MOTHER'S CHILDHOOD WAS
like growing up in the rural South during the 1940s and 1950s. As I sit
here now, reflecting on the stories she shared with me over the years,
I am struck by the strength and resilience she displayed from such
a young age. My mother, Sedonia Thomas, was born into a world of
poverty, hard work, and deep faith that would shape the course of her
life in ways she could never have imagined.

Mom entered this world on a warm day in 1945, in the small
town of Heth, Arkansas. She was the last of nine children born to her
mother and her biological father, a man she would never have the

chance to know. When Mom was just an infant, her father passed away, leaving her mother to care for the large family on her own. It was a difficult time, but my grandmother was a woman of unwavering faith and determination. She knew that she could not raise her children alone, so when Mom was still a little girl, her mother remarried a man named Clarence Wyatt.

Clarence, who would become the only father Mom ever knew, was a pastor and a man of great presence. He was known throughout the community as a big, intimidating figure, but to Mom, he was a loving and supportive stepfather. With Clarence, my grandmother had seven more children, bringing the total number of siblings to a staggering sixteen. It was a house full of love, laughter, and the occasional squabble, but through it all, they remained a tight-knit family. Growing up in rural Arkansas, life was not easy for Mom and her family. They were sharecroppers, working long hours in the cotton fields to make ends meet. Mom often spoke of how much she hated picking cotton, the hot sun beating down on her back as she dragged her heavy sack down the endless rows. "I remember my older brothers, they were always looking out for me," she would say with a smile. "They taught me all the tricks to make the work a little easier. We'd put dirt and rocks in our bags to make weight faster. It was the only way to survive out there."

Despite the hardships, Mom's childhood was not without joy. She grew up surrounded by the love of her family and the strength of her faith. Clarence, as a pastor, made sure that his children were raised with a deep understanding of God's love and the importance of living a Christian life. Church was a central part of their lives, and Mom often spoke of the comfort and guidance she found in her faith, even from a young age.

As Mom entered her teenage years, she began to test the boundaries of her strict upbringing. She and her siblings would sneak out to visit nearby towns and clubs, eager to experience a taste of the world beyond their small community. She thought they were so clever she would laugh. But Grandpa Clarence always seemed to find out. He was a preacher, but he was no fool. When they got caught, Grandpa Clarence would sit them down and remind them of the importance of staying on the right path, his words a mix of sternness and love.

Despite the occasional rebelliousness, Mom was known throughout the family as the caring, mild-mannered peacekeeper. She had a special bond with each of her siblings, a connection that would last a lifetime. She was the one in the middle. The one that got along with everybody. I guess that was just her nature, to try and make sure everyone was happy. It was this nature that would be put to the test when, at the age of 17, Mom found herself unwed and pregnant. I heard many stories saying the father was a man by the name of Alfred, but my mother would neither deny nor confirm this rumor. However, a handsome man named Lonnie Hester, who had sought after my mom for years, didn't care that she was pregnant with another man's child. He just wanted to be with her. In the rural South of the 1960s, it was not uncommon for young women to start families early, but for Mom, it was a moment that would change the course of her life. She did not want to marry Lonnie but, not to bring shame to the family, her parents insisted. She knew deep down that it wasn't right. But back then, she didn't question her parents, nor did she want to be labeled as an unwed mother, so she did what was expected of her.

As she stood there, a young bride and a newborn, I knew that my mother held onto the hope and the faith that had carried her through so much already. She knew that God had a plan for her, and she was ready to face whatever challenges lay ahead. Preparing to leave the only home she had ever known and start a new life in the North, she carried with her the strength and the resilience that had been forged in the cotton fields of Arkansas. She was ready to begin the next chapter of her life.

As I sit here now, I can't help but marvel at the strength my mother showed, even in those early years. To be so young, to face so many challenges growing into adulthood and still maintain her loyalty and love for her family, is a testament to the woman she would become. Little did she know that this moment, this decision to marry Lonnie would set her on a path that would test her in ways she could never have imagined.

Chapter 2:

LIFE UP NORTH

ᖊᖊᖊᖊᖊᖊᖊ

*P*hilippians 4:19 (KJV): "But my God shall supply all your needs according to his riches in glory by Christ Jesus."

MOM WAS JUST SEVENTEEN WHEN SHE HAD MY BIG SISTER ZELDA in 1963. Still, practically a child herself, thrust into the world of motherhood before she even finished high school. But that's the way it often was for girls in the South back then. Childhood seemed to slip through their fingers, the realities of womanhood arriving swiftly and without warning.

At eighteen, Mom married the man who would later become my dad, Lonnie Hester. Their union came quickly on the heels of Zelda's birth, a whirlwind of adult responsibilities for a girl barely out of pigtails. I imagine Mom standing at the altar, her youthful face aglow with a mixture of nerves and naivete. Her stepfather, the only father she ever knew, was by her side to give her away. She respected him so; despite any misgivings she may have had about marrying Daddy.

Less than two years after the wedding, Mom found herself pregnant again. Another baby, another mouth to feed. My brother Terrance came into the world in 1965, his arrival marking a turning point in our family's story. It was around this time that Daddy's brothers up North started whispering in his ear about greener pastures. "Come on up to Davenport, Iowa," they said. "Plenty of jobs in the big factories. A chance to escape the limited prospects of the South."

So, with two babies in tow, Mom and Daddy packed up their meager belongings and set out for Davenport. Zelda was just a toddler, Terrence a tiny bundle. Mom's heart must have been heavy, leaving behind the only home she'd ever known to start a new life in the North. The beautiful Arkansas dirt seemed to flow through her very veins. Carrying with her the strength and resilience that had been forged in the cotton fields of Arkansas. But she did it for the promise of a better life, even if it meant venturing into the unknown.

Before they left, though, Mom had to grapple with the painful realities of the segregated South. She told me a story once, about her grandmother. Her grandmother had been working on a man's land when she got injured. The way Mom told it, she was owed some money or a piece of property as compensation. But the owner refused to pay up. Instead, he sent men to handle it. In the end, her grandmother was beheaded, and her body was never found.

Mom said it took a toll on the whole family. Not only did they have to endure the brutality of the murder, but Mom's twin brothers, just teenagers at the time, were accused of killing their own grandmother. That's the kind of injustice black folks faced in those days. It's no wonder Mom wanted out. She had her doubts as a human, but as she grew older and wiser, she started to understand that God doesn't play favorites. Black, white, red, green - it doesn't matter. What matters is the condition of your heart. And Mom, well, she had a forgiving spirit, even in the face of such cruelty.

Leaving the South behind, Mom thought she was escaping hardship. But Iowa brought its own set of challenges. Daddy struggled to hold down a job, his tenth-grade education proving a major hindrance. He'd get work here and there at the big industrial plants, but it never seemed to last. The frustration ate away at him, turning him mean and resentful.

Daddy had grown up dirt poor, never having much of anything. So, when he started making a little money, he wanted to spend it on himself. Flashy clothes, nights out drinking, material things he couldn't afford. Anything to make him feel like a big man, even if it meant his family went without. Mom would try to reason with him and remind him of the bills that needed paying. But he'd just brush her off, saying, "I'm gonna buy that item, who cares if the light bill's due."

Dad's selfishness became the center of the marriage. Playing on Mom's sympathy to avoid taking responsibility for his childish behavior. Questions turned to nagging and nagging into arguments. That's when the abuse started. At first, it was just words, sharp and cutting. Daddy would lash out at Mom, calling her all manner of names. He wanted to control her, make her feel small. But as the pressures mounted and the babies kept coming, his cruelty turned physical. A shove here, a slap there. Each blow chipping away at Mom's spirit bit by bit.

She hid the bruises well, especially from her stepfather back in Arkansas. Mom knew if he found out, there'd be hell to pay. He was fiercely protective of her, and the thought of anyone laying a hand on his baby girl would have sent him into a rage. Mom had a couple of sisters that joined her in Iowa. They would quickly learn of the abuse. They saw the way she flinched at sudden movements; the way she'd go quiet when Daddy was on a rampage.

One sister in particular, refused to stand by and watch. Built like a tank and just as tough, she'd come charging over whenever Daddy started in on Mom. "You better get your hands off Mickey!" she'd holler, using Mom's childhood nickname. The two of them would scrap like alley cats until Daddy finally slunk away, tail between his legs.

But even our aunt's interventions couldn't stop the cycle of abuse. By 1969, Mom had five little ones under the age of five and a husband who terrified her. She knew she couldn't go on like this, living in constant fear for herself and her babies. She decided to divorce dad and with the help of Daddy's uncle and brothers, she was able to escape the unimaginable life she had and never looked back.

I can only imagine the courage it took for Mom to strike out on her own. Five little ones clinging to her skirt, no real means of support. But she did it because staying was no longer an option. She put Daddy out and set about the daunting task of rebuilding a life for her fractured family.

As I reflect on this chapter of Mom's story, I'm struck by her quiet strength in the face of unimaginable adversity. Uprooted from all she knew, thrust into single motherhood, battered, and beaten down by the man she thought would cherish her. Lesser women would have crumbled under the weight of it all.

But not my mom. She dug deep within herself and found a well-spring of resilience, even if she didn't fully recognize it at the time.

It reminds me of that scripture she held so dear, Philippians 4:19. "But my God shall supply all your needs according to his riches in glory by Christ Jesus." Mom clung to those words like a lifeline, trusting that somehow, someway, the Lord would provide. And provide He did, though the path was never easy.

Mom thought she had escaped the nightmare of abuse when she divorced Daddy. She couldn't have known that history was about to repeat itself, the cycle of violence rearing its ugly head once more. A second marriage loomed on the horizon, one that would test the very limits of Mom's faith and fortitude. But that's a story for another day. For now, I'll rest in the knowledge that my mom was a survivor, long before she even knew the true depth of her own strength.

Chapter 3:

KNIGHT-MARE IN SHINING ARMOR

ممممممم

*P*salms 91:1 (KJV): "He that dwelleth in the secret place of the most High shall abide under the shadow of the Almighty."

MOM'S DIVORCE FROM MY BIOLOGICAL FATHER LONNIE WAS finalized in 1969 when I was less than a year old. She didn't remain single for long. Almost immediately after, through a mutual friend, she met a man named John Roland. To Mom, John seemed to offer everything she was looking for at the time - safety, security, and a chance to start anew.

John had a background that appeared impressive at first glance. Like Mom, he hailed from the South, specifically East St. Louis. He had served in the Navy and now, back in civilian life, he cut an attractive figure with his dark skin and strong build. I can only imagine how

YET WILL I TRUST HIM

John must have looked to Mom then, with the hurt from my father's mistreatment still fresh. Perhaps he seemed like a protector, a provider - a knight in shining armor who came to rescue her.

They wed quickly in 1970, mere months after Mom's divorce was finalized. I was just a toddler then, too young to understand the changes happening around me. But I remember, as I grew older, Mom telling me how deeply she had loved John in the beginning. She truly believed she had found her soulmate, the man who would love and cherish her the way she deserved.

Our family began to grow rapidly. Within a year of their marriage, my first little brother John Jr. was born - Mom's sixth child. She was thrilled. Motherhood was Mom's greatest joy, and she relished the feeling of cradling a new baby. Maybe, in the secret recesses of her heart, she hoped a child would cement her bond with my stepfather, John, forever. Surely, if he had a son to carry on his name, he would never abandon her.

But the fractures in their marriage began to show almost immediately. It soon became clear that my stepfather had a severe drinking problem - and when he drank, he transformed into a different person entirely. The kind, charming man Mom had married would vanish, replaced by a raging, violent tyrant who terrorized her verbally and physically.

It felt like a cruel replay of Mom's first marriage, the nightmare of abuse starting all over again. But this time, it was even more severe. John's beatings were brutal and merciless. He seemed to relish degrading and humiliating her.

Far too often, we children were witness to these vicious attacks. I vividly recall huddling in a corner with my siblings, watching in terror as John pummeled our mother until she fell to the ground. We were far too little and helpless to do anything but observe Mom's suffering.

Faced with such relentless abuse, I think many women would have broken. But not my mother. With a strength that still leaves me in awe to this day, she bore the immense burden of raising eight children amidst unimaginable turmoil and violence.

We lived in abject poverty, relying on welfare to help support us. I remember those times vividly. Many nights, the lights would be turned off because we couldn't afford the bill. But even in the midst of such hardship, Mom's incredible spirit shone through. She was a phenomenal cook, able to make the most humble ingredients feel like a gourmet feast. Her fried chicken was the best I've ever tasted, and her cornbread was heavenly. Even when all we had was a pot of vegetable soup because meat was too expensive, Mom made it delicious. As kids, we might have grumbled about eating beans or soup yet again, but looking back, I marvel at how Mom kept us nourished on so little.

Mom always managed to get food on the table, no matter how dire things seemed. She had an uncanny ability to stretch the most meager provisions into a meal that could feed us all. And when there was no food left to stretch, she would go hungry herself so that we could eat.

"You are my everything," she would say to us, gathering us close. "I would move heaven and earth to keep y'all safe."

And she did. Lord knows she did. When my stepdad's drunken rage turned violent, Mom would gather us up and flee to one of her sisters' houses. They lived close by, thank the Lord, and they never turned us away no matter the hour. I remember the terror of those flights, all of us in our pajamas piled into the station wagon, Mom's face bruised and swollen but her jaw set with determination.

My aunts were momma bears when it came to protecting Mom. They never hesitated to confront my stepdad head-on, getting right in his face and giving him a piece of their mind. More times than I could count, I saw my aunts exchange blows with my stepdad right out in the street in front of our house. Knowing Mom had her sisters to depend on was a small comfort. But it didn't put an end to the abuse. Nothing did.

Maybe that's why, in the midst of all this chaos, Mom made a decision that might seem unfathomable to some. In rapid succession after John Jr., she had two more babies with my stepfather - my little brother Jeri and sister Sophia. Looking at it from an outsider's perspective, it wouldn't make sense. Why bring more children into such a volatile home life? But I understand Mom's reasoning. To her, every baby was a blessing, a tiny bundle of hope and possibility. Each new child was a fresh beginning, another shot at the loving family she yearned for so badly. And maybe, in her heart of hearts, she thought if she just loved my stepdad enough, if she just gave him enough children, he would transform. He would finally become the husband and father she knew he had the potential to be.

It was a desperate fantasy; I know that now. Magical thinking born out of trauma and pain. But it was that hope that carried Mom through some of the darkest periods of her life. When my stepdad went on a rampage, when he left her battered and broken, she would go inside herself and dream of a brighter tomorrow. A future where her babies were protected and cherished, where she was loved and valued.

During those brutal, unending years married to John, that future must have felt impossibly out of reach. But Mom's hope never wavered. Even as the abuse escalated and the babies kept arriving, her faith in the marriage remained steadfast and resolute.

And ultimately, it was that deep and abiding faith that gave Mom the strength to make the most consequential choice of her life - to finally break free from John's abuse and dedicate her life wholly to God.

But that chapter of Mom's story will have to wait. For now, what's important to understand is that even in her darkest hours, suffering degradation and torment that would have destroyed a lesser person, my mother never forgot who she was at her core - a beloved daughter of God, worthy of love and respect. That fundamental truth would be her North Star, guiding her through the storms to come and ultimately leading her to a life of purpose and peace.

In the chapters ahead, we will see how Mom's ironclad faith became a lodestar, giving her the courage to shatter the cycle of abuse and construct a new existence for herself and her children. As she embarked on a profound spiritual odyssey, she came to see that God had a divine plan for her all along - to alchemize her pain into purpose and transform her into a living testimony of hope for countless others.

Chapter 4:

TURNING TO GOD

∽∽∽∿∽∽∽

ebrews 12:2 (KJV): "Looking unto Jesus the author and finisher of our faith; who for the joy that was set before him endured the cross, despising the shame, and is set down at the right hand of the throne of God."

IN THE YEAR 1972, MOM'S LIFE TOOK A PROFOUND TURN, A glimmer of hope amidst the chaos and pain that had engulfed our family. The abuse from my stepfather John had reached new heights of cruelty, leaving us all reeling in its wake. But it was in this darkest of times that a lifeline was extended, an invitation that would change the course of Mom's life forever. Her uncle on John's side of the family, a beacon of light in the darkness, asked her to visit Pentecostal Deliverance Church where he attended. With a heavy heart and a desperate need for solace, Mom accepted.

I wasn't quite five yet but I remember the first time she walked through those church doors, like a wilted flower beaten down by the storms of life. But as she crossed the threshold, I watched in awe as a transformation began to take place. Giving her fragile life to Christ, the weight of the world seemed to lift from her shoulders, and a flicker of light ignited in her eyes. It was as if she had found a sanctuary, a place where she could finally breathe.

From that moment on, Mom threw herself into every aspect of church life. She became a fixture at every service, every activity, every opportunity to serve. It was like watching a phoenix rise from the ashes as she found new purpose and meaning in her faith. The church became her lifeline, a place where she could escape the horrors of home and immerse herself in the love and grace of God.

But even as Mom's faith blossomed, the darkness at home continued to fester. In 1975, when I was just a little girl, Mom made the heart-wrenching decision to divorce John. It was a time of great upheaval for our family as we struggled to find our footing in a world turned upside down. But Mom remained steadfast in her faith, clinging to the promises of God like a lifeline in a storm-tossed sea.

And then, in 1977, a miracle happened. John, the man who had caused so much pain and suffering, walked through the doors of the church. He claimed to have changed, to have found God and turned over a new leaf. Mom, with her heart full of hope and her eyes fixed on Jesus, decided to give him another chance. They remarried, and for a brief moment, it seemed like everything would be okay.

But the change in John was short-lived. I always wondered if he only changed to win her back. Before long, the old patterns of abuse and destruction re-emerged, and Mom found herself once again in the clutches of a man consumed by darkness. But this time, something was different. Mom had found a new strength, a new resilience born of her deep and abiding faith in God.

She rededicated her life to the Lord and threw herself even more fully into the church community. It became her refuge, her sanctuary, the one place where she could find peace and purpose amidst the chaos of her life. Mom stopped wearing pants, never cut her hair, and eschewed makeup, all in accordance with the teachings of her new pastor. Some might have seen these changes as restrictive, but for Mom, they were a badge of honor, a sign of her complete devotion to God.

Her gifts and talents began to shine like never before. She became the choir director, pouring her heart and soul into every hymn and chorus. She taught Sunday school, sharing the love of Jesus with the little ones who flocked to her like moths to a flame. She joined the Love & Care committee, reaching out to those in need with a heart full of compassion and grace.

But Mom's service didn't stop there. She helped lead prayer meetings, Bible studies, and choir rehearsals. She volunteered for community vacation Bible school and took on any task, no matter how small or menial, with a heart full of joy and a spirit of humility. It was as if she had found her true calling, her reason for being.

And through it all, Mom found a kindred spirit in her best friend Lorraine. The two women became inseparable, sharing their hearts and their burdens with a bond that could only be forged in the fires of adversity. Lorraine became Mom's closest confidant, the one person she could turn to when the weight of the world became too much to bear.

But even as Mom's faith soared to new heights, the darkness at home continued to fester. My stepdad, threatened by the amount of time she was spending at church, lashed out with a vengeance. He would beat her in public, trying to prevent her from leaving the house.

He came to church threatening to drag her out if she did not leave. Having come home one Friday night after church, we discovered he had destroyed everything in our home. TVs were busted, furniture was slashed, dishes and mirrors were broken; the house was as if a tornado had whirled through during one of his fits of drunken rage. All because Mom refused to give in to his demands. I could see the disappointment and pain in her eyes, but she never grumbled once. She grabbed the broom and asked us to help clean up the damage. She covered the couch with blankets and salvaged all she could to make the home as presentable as possible. How could the man that professed his love to her destroy the very home where we as little ones laid our heads?

As a child, I couldn't wrap my head around it. How could Mom keep believing in a God that let such terrible things happen? How could she pray to a Father in heaven when her husband on earth treated her so deplorably?

But with the benefit of hindsight and maturity, I see now the incredible fortitude in Mom's unshakeable faith. It was her guiding light in the darkness, an anchor that kept her from drowning even in her most despairing moments. It was this resiliency that I knew my mom was special.

Through it all, Mom never complained. She never brought her troubles to church, never let on to the other members the hell she was living at home. Instead, she focused on her ministry, on the work God had called her to do. She poured herself into the lives of others, offering hope and healing to those who were hurting, all while bearing the weight of her own unspeakable pain.

Her faith only grew stronger. She became a prayer warrior, a woman of deep spiritual gifts and unwavering devotion to God. She would spend hours on her knees, crying out to the Lord for strength and guidance. And even when the storms of life threatened to over-whelm her, she never lost sight of the One who had called her out of darkness and into His marvelous light.

Looking back now, I can see how much Mom sacrificed for her faith. She spent nearly 60-70% of her time each week dedicated to church activities, pouring herself out like a drink offering before the Lord. She hid the abuse she suffered at home, bearing the burden alone so as not to tarnish the testimony of God's goodness in her life. Persevering, she remained a glimmer of hope and light to all who knew her.

As I reflect on those years, I am filled with awe and wonder at the strength of my mother's faith. She endured unspeakable hardship and pain, yet never wavered in her devotion to God. She clung to Jesus like a drowning man clings to a life raft, and in doing so, she found the strength to keep going, to keep loving, to keep serving.

And now, as I look ahead to the next chapter of her story, I am filled with a sense of anticipation and hope. For I know that even in the darkest of times, even when the road ahead seems impossibly hard, Mom's faith will be her guiding light. She will continue to walk in the footsteps of Jesus, her eyes fixed on the joy set before her, no matter what trials and tribulations may come

For that is the legacy of Sedonia Hester-Roland a woman whose faith was forged in the fires of affliction, and whose love for God knew no bounds. And it is a legacy that will live on, long after she has passed from this earth and into the arms of her Savior.

In the next chapter, we will delve deeper into the challenges Mom faced as she sought to live out her faith in the midst of unimag-inable adversity. We will see how her unwavering commitment to

God sustained her through the darkest of times, and how her example continues to inspire and encourage us all to this day.

Chapter 5:

LIFE OF FAITH
DURING HARDSHIP

∿∿∿∿∿

Romans 8:38-39 (KJV): "For I am persuaded, that neither death, nor life, nor angels, nor principalities, nor powers, nor things present, nor things to come, nor height, nor depth, nor any other creature, shall be able to separate us from the love of God, which is in Christ Jesus our Lord."

AS THE LATE 1970S MELTED INTO THE 1980S, I WATCHED IN AWE as my mother's faith only seemed to grow stronger, even as the waves of adversity crashed relentlessly against the shores of our family life. Mom's unwavering devotion to God was like a beacon of light, guiding us through the darkest of storms.

John, my stepfather, had briefly tasted the sweetness of redemption, dipping his toes in the waters of faith. But like a moth drawn to a flame, he couldn't resist the siren call of his old ways. The bottle beckoned, and with it, the demons of abuse and control that had haunted our family for so long. It was a bitter pill to swallow, watching the man who had pledged to love and cherish my mother succumb to the darkness within him.

But my stepdad wasn't alone in his struggle. His family, a web of enablers and co-conspirators, seemed hell-bent on dragging him back into the abyss. Every time he stumbled, they were there to offer a drink and a pat on the back, as if to say, "This is who you really are." It broke my heart to see my mother's hopes for a better life dashed time and time again.

Yet, in the face of this unrelenting adversity, Mom's faith only burned brighter. It was as if each trial, each setback, only served to stoke the flames of her devotion. I watched in amazement as she began to stand up to my stepdad's attempts at control, armed with nothing more than the armor of God and the unshakable conviction that He was by her side.

It was during this time that my mother's connection with the divine seemed to deepen to an almost supernatural degree. Her discernment, her ability to sense God's presence and guidance in even the most mundane of events, was uncanny. It was as if she had a direct line to the heavens, and the miracles that followed in her wake were too numerous to count.

I remember one particularly trying time when there was nothing left in the house to eat. But Mom never wavered or worried. She simply said, "That's okay. God said we're going to eat today." And just like that, there was a car honking outside. It was a lady from our church, declaring, "Hey Sister Roland, God just told me to come over and bring these bags of groceries to you." Just out of the blue, without any prompting from my mother. She knew it was God directly providing for our needs, blessing those who were faithful to Him.

And then there was the time when my mother desperately needed to pay a bill but had no money whatsoever. She went into prayer, saying, "I don't know how we're gonna make it through this God, but you know, work it out." And while she was praying, God told her to go into her closet, to a particular jacket, and reach into the pocket. There, she found two crisp $100 bills, just enough to pay the bill that was due. These were the kinds of miracles that we witnessed over and over as kids, but at the time, we didn't fully understand or appreciate the magnitude of what was happening. It was simply an expectation, a part of how we grew up in the church.

I remember one hot summer day, my mom and her sisters decided to take all the children to Niabi Zoo for the day. After relentless hours of family fun, my aunts wanted to take the kids to Credit Island, a man-made beach, to wade in the water. As we were traveling down the highway, each car following the other, my mom began to hunk her horn to get my aunt's attention in their cars. When they finally pulled to the side of the road my mom walks up to the other cars and told my aunts, "God said to take my kids home" and commanded all of us to get in her car. I recall my brothers and I were upset and felt Mom was keeping us from having fun. As I think back on everything now, I realize the close relationship she had with God and her ability to recognize, listen, and obey His voice. Not even a couple of hours after separating from the rest of the family, my mom and I were returning from the corner store after picking up her RC Cola when a carload of church members pulled up. They were honking the car horn trying to get my mom's attention before we walked in the house. They immediately began asking her if she had heard the news. She asked, "What news?" They asked again if she had heard. Oblivious as to what they were asking, my mom walked up to their car and once again asked what they were referring to. They then began to notify her that there was a story on the local news stating that one of her sister's kids had drowned. My mom's sister lived a block down the street, so my mom and I jumped in her car and drove to my aunt's house. Upon arrival, we were met by many neighborhood friends, the police and the news cast surrounding the yard. I was amazed at the number of folks crowding my aunt's yard. My mom made her way into the house but made me and several other of my siblings stay in the yard. She came back outside eventually with teary eyes to notify us that my Aunt Ruth had lost all 4 of her kids due to drowning in the Mississippi River. I was flabbergasted even at 10 years old. I didn't understand what was happening. One minute I'm at the zoo with my cousins, ranging in age from 2 to 13, having a great time and the next minute they were gone forever. I vividly remember attending the funeral with four caskets lined across the pulpit of the church. The pain on my aunt's face while sitting in the front row glaring at each one, as if each child would rise and walk, one by one. My siblings and I asked our mom why God would allow this to happen. How could she explain this devastating event to her own kids who couldn't grasp what just happened? I vaguely remember her saying that she doesn't have the answer, but we don't question God's decision. She then went on to say God preferred to have them all with Him. I'm not sure my mom truly understood herself how to explain it to us but even in her pain, she was there to comfort us and ensure us that God doesn't make mistakes. It's hard to comprehend even to this day but I now realize that had my mother not listened to the voice of God, that could have been me or any of my brothers and sisters drowning in that river on that day.

As Mom poured herself into mentoring the youth at our church, modeling what it meant to live a virtuous, upright Christian life, trouble began brewing closer to home. Two of my older brothers began to dabble in drugs and run with the wrong crowd, while my younger sister found herself rebelling, eventually leading to her becoming pregnant while still a teenager. It was a heavy cross to bear, but my mother shouldered it with grace and compassion, determined to support her children through every trial.

Even within the walls of our church, Mom faced opposition from small-minded women who seemed to resent the anointing that God had so clearly bestowed upon her. They whispered behind her back, questioning her motives and casting aspersions on her character. But my mother, in her infinite wisdom, chose to meet their hostility with love and understanding. "You may see the price," she once told me, tears brimming in her eyes, "but you don't know the cost it took me to get here."

And yet, as she traveled the region, preaching the gospel and leading revivals, Mom kept her own troubles locked away, hidden from the countless souls she touched. She was a master of compartmentalization, able to set aside her own suffering for the sake of those who needed her most.

Back at home, my mother's faith was put to the test on a daily basis. My stepdad's abuse, both verbal and physical, showed no signs of abating, but Mom refused to be cowed. She would march out the door every Sunday, head held high, even as he raged and threatened. It was a quiet act of defiance, a declaration that her allegiance was to a higher power.

I recall the biggest test of faith came after a violent night of my stepfather's rage. My mom once again ran with her children. She found refuge at her sister's small one bedroom apartment. My stepfather showed up at my aunt's house seeking her out, with the rage and intention to kill her. I recall how God was able to protect and shield her from the storm that came her way. My aunt stalled my stepfather until my mother could hide in the bathroom of her apartment once Mom had secured all but the 2 youngest of her kids in the back bedroom. I recall hearing my stepfather's loud scary voice while hiding in the back. After my aunt kept refusing to let him in, my stepfather, the cunning person he is, then asked to use the restroom. Hesitant to let him in, my aunt had no choice. Not allowing him in would indicate my mother was in the apartment. Once he entered the apartment, he began searching each closet, and the bedroom. Unable to find her, he turned to leave and told my aunt, "Tell that "B** when I catch her, I'm going to kill her." Realizing he still needed to use the restroom he reversed his path and proceeded to go towards the restroom door. My aunt looked in horror but did not want to give away the fact that my mom was hiding in the restroom. As my stepfather walks into the restroom where my mom is hiding, I remember her saying all she could do was pray for God's blood to cover her.

As my stepfather finished his business in the restroom and began to walk out the door, he quickly turned back to slide open the glass shower door, taking one last peak to see if my mom was hiding in the tub. My mom stated she could see him, but he never saw her with my two younger siblings lying on her chest. Somehow, someway, God had shielded her or blinded my stepfather such that he never saw her when she was right in front of his eyes. As a young girl, I knew there was something different about my mom but didn't truly grasp the magnitude of the relationship she had with God until I saw before my own eyes, the supernatural miracles that were occurring over and over again. It was as if my mom was back in the biblical days where Jesus was manifesting his powers of healing the sick and raising the dead. This time however, my mom was one of the individuals Jesus decided to use and offer His grace and favor to. Like Peter, the disciple, my mom would also put down her net and follow Him and become a fisherman of souls. Never to look back.

Through it all—the poverty, the pain, the seemingly endless cycle of abuse—my mother's trust in God never wavered. It was a rock-solid foundation, a wellspring of strength that sustained her through even the darkest of days. When I asked her how she could remain so steadfast in the face of such adversity, her answer was simple yet profound: "I cannot waver, for my faith is not in man, but in God."

And so, she pressed on, finding joy in the small blessings that peppered her life—the laughter of her children, the warmth of our church community, the quiet moments of communion with her Heavenly Father. Mom was a living embodiment of the fruits of the Spirit, radiating love, joy, peace, patience, kindness, goodness, faithfulness, gentleness, and self-control to all who crossed her path.

Even when my stepdad made the decision to separate from her in 1982, choosing to live with his long-term girlfriend and returning to our home only when it suited him, my mother remained a pillar of forgiveness and grace. She knew, deep in her heart, that her true husband was the One who had sacrificed His life on the cross, and that no earthly separation could ever sever that bond.

As I reflect on those years, I am struck by the sheer significance of my mother's faith. It was a light in the darkness, a beacon of hope in a world that often seemed determined to snuff it out. Little did I know that the greatest test of Mom's faith was still to come, as the specter of illness loomed on the horizon, threatening to tear our world asunder. But even in the face of this ultimate trial, I knew that my mother would stand firm, a testament to the power of unwavering belief in the face of impossible odds.

Chapter 6:

FACING DEATH WITH FAITH

∽∿∿∿∿

*P*hilippians 1:21 (KJV): "For to me to live is Christ, and to die is gain."

AS I REFLECT ON THE FINAL CHAPTER OF MY MOTHER'S EXTRAOR-dinary life, I am struck by the unwavering strength of her faith, even as her body succumbed to the ravages of cancer. It was in the late 1980s, while I was away at college, that Mom received the devastating diagnosis of advanced cervical cancer. Initially, she kept the news mostly to herself, not wanting to burden us children with worry. But as her condition deteriorated, the truth could no longer be hidden.

I vividly remember calling my mother one day and asking her how she was feeling. She franticly asked, "Who told you, who told you?" I had no idea what she was referring to, so I politely asked, "Told me what?" Because she let the cat out of the bag with her response, she had no choice but to fill me in. Her response brought my world to a short standstill, although I was still unsure of the magnitude of what she was saying. The doctors had found cells in her cervix requiring them to go in and scrape her uterus. I was not a medical doctor and accepted her response obliviously.

Mom was a powerful woman of faith so I had no doubt she would bounce back from whatever she was dealing with. So much so, she still came to the university I attended to speak one last time. This time she brought several young ladies in the choir along with my brother and younger sister. During this particular visit, she didn't want to stay in the hotel they had reserved for her, but instead wanted to stay in my dorm room with me to mingle with the young ladies I knew. I gave my mother the weekend of a lifetime by allowing her to live in my world for a day; touring the campus, eating in the school cafeteria, and meeting many students that crossed her path. She enjoyed every minute of it. It was during this visit that I also noticed the continuous bleeding my mother was experiencing. I did not question anything as I assumed it was her monthly cycle which is a common occurrence for women. The thought of my indomitable mother, the epitome of vitality and resilience, facing any such illness would be too much to bear. Especially after hearing her preach a powerful message to the students during the Sunday service. Many students felt God's presence through her that day. Flooding the alter, breaking down in tears, and surrendering their life to Christ. After service, so many approached her, sharing how her message had touched them to the core. Mom had an uncanny ability to precisely deliver the nuggets of hope and truth each person desperately needed to hear. Her words carried weight because she didn't just preach them - she lived them out daily in her own radical obedience and utter dependence on the Lord. At that moment I felt my mother was a vessel that could not be broken. So, it came with shock when I received a phone call from my oldest sister months after Mom had returned home saying she was not feeling well and stayed home from church. I knew at that moment, whatever she was going through was serious as my mother would never miss an engagement at church, especially a Sunday service. I was informed my mom had cancer, so I raced home from school, desperate to be by her side. When I arrived, I was not prepared mentally for what stood on the other side of the front door when she opened it. The frail frame she had become shook me to my core. How could this be? I had just seen her months before full of life, healthy and strong. Could this really be the same vibrant woman who had raised eight children with such grace and fortitude?

But then Mom met my gaze with those clear steady eyes that always seemed to penetrate my very soul. "Don't you worry, now," she reassured me with a calm smile. "I know God is going to heal me completely. I have faith." Even in the face of death, her trust in the Lord remained unshakable.

When the doctors recommended surgery and a hysterectomy to combat the cancer, Mom refused. She was steadfast in her belief that God would deliver her from this trial, that He would restore her to wholeness without the need for medical intervention. Some might have called it foolhardy, but I recognized it as an extension of the profound faith she had nurtured through a lifetime of adversity.

And so, Mom pressed on, enduring bouts of excruciating pain but never losing her grip on God's promises. Remarkably, she continued to pour herself into ministry, even as she fought for her very life. She traveled to preach when standing was an almost insurmountable challenge, and she counseled church members and strangers alike, offering them comfort and inspiration in their own times of need.

I watched in awe as she delivered her final testimony at church, mere weeks before the cancer consumed her body. "I have fought a good fight, I have finished my course, I have kept the faith," she proclaimed, quoting II Timothy 4:8 in that powerful, unwavering voice. "Henceforth there is laid up for me a crown of righteousness, which the Lord, the righteous judge, shall give me on that day." The congregation wept and shouted, praising God for this courageous woman of faith. Mom raised her hands in exultation, her face radiant with joy. It was the last time she would physically enter the doors of the church.

Shortly after, she collapsed at home and was placed in at- home hospice care as the end drew near. By 1991, we all knew that her transition from this earthly life to her eternal reward was imminent. Mom gathered us children to her bedside in those final days, ensuring that each one of us felt the depth of her love and the pride she had in the individuals we had become.

Even in her last hours, she was not spared the cruelty and abuse that had cast a shadow over her marriage. I will never forget overhearing my stepfather's final confrontation with her, as she lay on what would become her deathbed. My stepfather, after one of his many nights out, returned home drunk, smelling of liquor. As he entered the room where my mom was resting, my mother asked him to leave because the smell of alcohol was making her nauseated. Still trying to break her soul, he lashed back at her saying, "You about to die anyway b****, so who gives a f*** about you feeling sick." His words dripping with venom and bitterness pierced the very depth of her soul. For the first time since being sick, I saw quiet tears flow down her face. Forever unshakable in her faith, Mom simply turned her eyes heavenward and said, "Though he slayed me, yet will I trust Him."

The secret resentment she had towards my stepfather was made known in a dream she had a few weeks later. She told us that in her dream she went to Heaven, but God would not let her through the pearly gates. She didn't understand why after all she had done on earth to serve Him. She went down the list naming the many things she had accomplished only to hear God tell her he would not let her in because of the hate she harbored towards my stepfather. After she had awakened from the dream, she knew she needed to find forgiveness for the very man that made her life hell on earth. She wrote a long letter to my stepfather asking him to forgive her, then requested my older sister to take it to him. With this letter she had made her peace, forgiving every wrong he did, trusting that God would be her ultimate vindicator. And in the end, it was not the face of her tormentor that she focused on, but the face of her Savior. Not long after writing this letter, Mom fell into a coma.

When Mom finally took her last breath, it was with a beatific smile gracing her lips. I have never seen a more joyful, peaceful expression on any person, living or dead. It was as if she was already catching a glimpse of the glory that awaited her in the life to come. "Well done, my good and faithful servant," I could almost hear God whisper as He welcomed her into His loving embrace at last.

The funeral was a testament to the countless lives Mom had touched. It was probably the largest funeral I have ever witnessed. The church was so packed that people were spilling out the doors. The windows of the church had to be opened so those waiting outside could hear the service. Instead of wearing the traditional black color for the funeral, my siblings and I decided to wear white in celebration of Mom's pure, innocent, and sacrificial life.

I remember my brother getting up to sing one of her favorite songs, "When I see Jesus," his voice cracking with emotion. And as I stood by her casket, gazing at her serene face, I was struck by how happy she looked. It was as if she was saying, "I have made it. I am truly happy now." Even in death, her joy was palpable. The procession seemed to stretch on for miles, with people I hadn't seen in years, some who didn't even attend our church, coming to pay their respects. I recall the police blocking traffic and people standing on the sidewalks showing their respect. Strangers stood on the outside of their cars, taking off their hats, and some even saluting as the hearse passed by. Never had I seen anything like it.

The wake, held the day before the funeral, was a beautiful tribute to Mom's legacy. I couldn't help but marvel at the peaceful smile that graced her features. It was a stark contrast to the anguished expression I saw on my aunt's face when she passed several years later. My aunt, who had once told Mom that Heaven was on earth, looked as though she had seen the very demons of hell as she took her last breath. But Mom? She looked as though she was already basking in the glory of her eternal reward.

As we laid Mom to rest, we knew that her impact would continue to ripple through generations. And while we, her children, knew we had to forgive our stepfather to truly honor her example, it was a difficult and painful journey. Mom had always taught us that bitterness and resentment would only poison our own souls in the end, and so we slowly, painstakingly worked to make peace with the past.

Not a day goes by that we don't feel Mom's absence acutely. But we also feel her presence, urging us onward, encouraging us to cling to our faith just as she did. Through every trial and storm, every cruel blow that life may deal, we know she is still with us, cheering us on to victory.

Now, as I reflect on the rich tapestry of faith and fortitude that was my mother's life, I am compelled to explore the ways in which her legacy continues to shape our family and our community. In the next chapter, we will delve into how Mom's memory and example live on, guiding us as we navigate an uncertain world with the same unwavering faith and devotion to God's purpose that defined her remarkable journey.

Chapter 7:

A LEGACY LIKE NO OTHER

༄༅༄༅༄

*J*ohn 14:27 (KJV): "Peace I leave with you, my peace
I give unto you: not as the world giveth, give I unto
you. Let not your heart be troubled, neither let it be afraid."

AS I REFLECT ON THE EXTRAORDINARY LIFE OF MY BELOVED
mother Sedonia, I am filled with an overwhelming sense of gratitude
and awe. Despite enduring unimaginable hardships - an early preg-
nancy, two abusive marriages, crushing poverty, and ultimately a
terminal illness - Mom's unwavering faith in God and her indomitable
spirit never faltered. She had a remarkable ability to focus solely on
her blessings, like her cherished family and church community, rather
than dwelling on the myriads of burdens she carried.

Through her everyday actions and very essence, Mom exem-
plified the highest of virtues - unconditional love, unshakable faith,
radical forgiveness, and selfless service to others. Her trust in the Lord
was so deeply ingrained, that it remained steadfast even when faced

with the severest of trials that would cause most to question their beliefs. I remember asking her once how she maintained such resolute faith despite the relentless abuse she suffered. She replied simply yet powerfully, "I cannot waver."

Those three small words carried immense weight and conviction. Mom drew her strength from an unassailable belief that God would never forsake her, even if His plans were sometimes difficult for our human minds to comprehend. This bedrock faith shaped the trajectory of not only her life but the lives of her eight children as well.

Growing up, we didn't have much in the way of material possessions. Most months were a struggle to keep the lights on and food on the table for so many hungry mouths to feed. But what Mom lacked in earthly resources, she more than made up for in spiritual wealth which she generously poured out on us. Scriptures and gospel music constantly filled our home, grounding us in Christian morals and values from a tender young age.

As we grew older and began making our own choices, not all of us stayed on the straight and narrow path Mom worked so tirelessly to set us on. We all experienced our share of worldly temptations for a season, and for some, continue to choose the world over Christ. But even when we strayed, Mom's fierce love and dedication to us never wavered. She continued interceding fervently for each lost sheep, trusting that her unrelenting faith and the seeds of righteousness she had sown would ultimately guide them back to the fold. And one by one, although she may not have witnessed those earnest prayers answered, God is still answering them as some have found their way home again. It's just a matter of time before all eight of her children will be back to where it started.

While our family was undoubtedly her heart, the church was Mom's lifeblood. She invested countless hours into her ministry - directing the choir, teaching Sunday school, opening the sanctuary each morning in prayer, counseling members, preparing meals for the congregation, and so much more. Despite our own lack, Mom always found a way to give what little we had to support our pastor and meet the needs she saw around her.

This radical generosity flowed from her deep wellspring of love for both God and people. Mom possessed a rare gift to make anyone feel seen, valued, and uplifted in her presence. Her bold, authentic faith was magnetic, drawing people from all walks of life to seek out her wise counsel and powerful prayers. She was never too busy to lend a listening ear, offer sage advice, or envelop a hurting soul in a comforting embrace.

I witnessed the profound impact of Mom's love firsthand by the many children that would frequent our home each Sunday after church. Our home was the home to go to every week. Dozens of church kids would crowd my mom after service each Sunday asking to come over to our house. She never said no. The church bus would empty completely when it pulled up to my house, with 16 to 20 kids unloading. Even with the little we had she was willing to share with everyone. She took them all under her wings, spreading joy and love to each one of them.

Even as she neared the end of her earthly journey, while cancer ravaged her body, Mom's faith and love burned brighter than ever. She pressed on in serving at church and pouring into others while simultaneously fighting her own excruciating battle. When it became clear that physical healing would not come in the way we had so desperately prayed for and clung to, she humbly submitted to God's will, trusting in His perfect plan and the promise of ultimate healing that awaited her in eternity.

The immense crowd that gathered to celebrate Mom's life and homegoing was a testament to the countless lives she had touched. As I looked out at the overflowing sanctuary and seemingly endless line of cars in the funeral procession stretching as far as the eye could see, I was struck by the beautiful legacy she had left behind.

It was one of resilience in the face of adversity, unshakable faith in God's goodness and sovereignty, sacrificial love for others, and the steadfast assurance that a life poured out in service to the Lord is never wasted.

In the painful years since her passing, I have clung to the many invaluable lessons Mom imparted to me, both through her words and perhaps more powerfully, her daily example. To run to God as my refuge and strength when my own inevitable strength fails me. To extend forgiveness freely just as I have been forgiven much. To trust in His unfailing provision when resources run scarce. To treat all people with Christ-like compassion, dignity, and love. And to live each day with eyes fixed on eternity, storing up imperishable treasures in Heaven rather than chasing fulfillment in temporary earthly things. But of all the wisdom she imparted, Mom's life taught me that our true purpose is ultimately found in loving God and loving people. She embodied this so consistently and wholeheartedly, staying anchored to her true north no matter how violently the storms of life raged around her. By keeping her gaze locked on Jesus, the author and perfecter of her faith, she was able to walk on the waves that threatened to overwhelm her.

Mom, although I miss you more with each passing day, I am eternally grateful for the rich spiritual inheritance you left behind. You taught me how to weather life's trials with grit and grace. You showed me what it means to forgive, to love unconditionally, and to serve with humility. Your unshakeable faith in the face of unthinkable hardship has become my anchor. Thank you for always pointing me back to Christ, my firm foundation when all else fails. I pray I can honor your memory by walking out this legacy of devotion until the day I see you again on the other side. You are so deeply loved.

If there was one thing Mom excelled at, even with extremely limited means, it was making us feel cherished on our birthdays. With five of her eight children born in the span of a few weeks in November, she was determined that each one would have their special moment to shine amidst the chaos of so many celebrations.

Despite the meager groceries that had to stretch impossibly far, Mom would labor for hours in the kitchen, whipping up each child's favorite meal and carefully crafting unique birthday cakes, no matter how bare the cupboards. For that one day, she ensured we knew just how precious we were in her eyes.

I have no doubt that my thoughtful, family-oriented mother is still celebrating birthdays in Heaven, no longer weighed down by the burdens, lack and afflictions she endured on earth. I picture her at a grand, lavished banquet table, surrounded by the many loved ones who went before her, feasting in the presence of her Savior. The spread is bountiful beyond description - every delicacy imaginable - because there is no more scarcity, only the abundance of God's riches in glory. And at each seat, a personalized cake, but this time one that will never run out, just as His mercies are new every morning.

Until we are reunited at that glorious feast, I will continue to celebrate her life and the truly priceless gifts she gave me - an eternal perspective, an unshakable foundation of faith, and a steadfast commitment to serving God no matter the earthly cost. This is my mother's enduring legacy. And I will spend the rest of my days striving to walk in the immense footsteps of faith she left behind. Well done, Mom. Well done.

PHOTO GALLERY

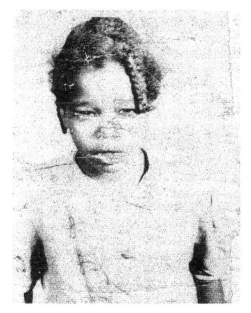

Mom as a little girl in Arkansas

Mom as a young adult in the south

My dad and my siblings

Mom marrying my stepdad

Mom and stepdad at church

Mom and Stepdad plus all 8 kids

Mom dressed for church

Mom relaxing at home

Mom attending an event at church

Mom preparing the choir for Sunday service

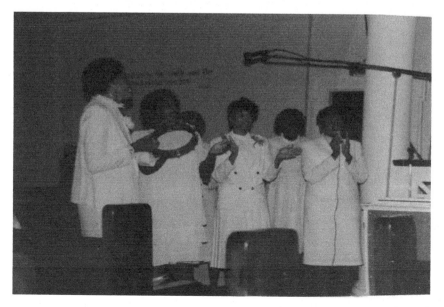

Mom singing in Women's program at church

Mom teaching Sunday school

Mom preaching a sermon

The last engagement my mom had where she preached at my university

Mom home during her illness

HOMEGOING CELEBRATION

FOR – AND

IN LOVING MEMORY

OF

Missionary Sedonia Thomas Roland

SERVICES

August 21, 1945   October 18, 1991

Thursday, October 24, 1991

1:00 P.M.

Eld. James E. Lee, Pastor

PENTECOSTAL DELIVERANCE CHURCH

636 Kirkwood Boulevard, Davenport, Iowa

ACKNOWLEDGEMENT

I want to give thanks to all those who helped make this book a success. First to my ride or die sisters, Zelda, Sophia, and Lonnette, my fabulous cousins, Tamara and Sharon and newfound friend Lenore. Thank you for being with me at our first Woman Evolve conference together where Pastor Sarah Jakes prophesied that by the same time next year, God would birth new things out of folks. My birthing process began immediately after the conference, as I knew it was time for me to move forward with what God had placed in my heart years before.

I also want to thank my heavenly Father for who he is - A way maker, miracle worker, promise keeper, light in my darkness. He has proven himself over and over again, so how can I not serve him for the rest of my life.

Lastly, I want to thank my brother, Lonnie Jr, for the words he can write so meaningfully and eloquently in poems and short stories. His talent far outweighs where he's been.

SISTER ROLAND

On this day I think of you
And that sunny day you died
The scorching heat, all that grief
And still, I didn't cry

I just bowed my head and closed my eyes
Hail Mary full of Grace
Cause, I know she cried those tears of joy
When she saw those pearly gates

God called her name and gave her wings
To walk those streets of gold
So don't worry 'bout what's left behind
Cuz your eight can hold their own

So, sing and dance and praise the Lord
And cry those tears of joy
Then lean in close when you're with God
And put a word in for your boy

You earned those wings so show them off
Spread them far and wide
You're surely missed, I send a kiss
With my prayers and a smile

Love you, Mom!